Izzy's New Life

The Way I Talk

Written, Illustrated & Designed

Latoy ... lfcn

ISBN: 978-1- 0420-13-9

After moving to Canada with her aunt Theresa, Izzy has to start school the following day.

She's in a new country and is excited about the new experiences she's about to have.

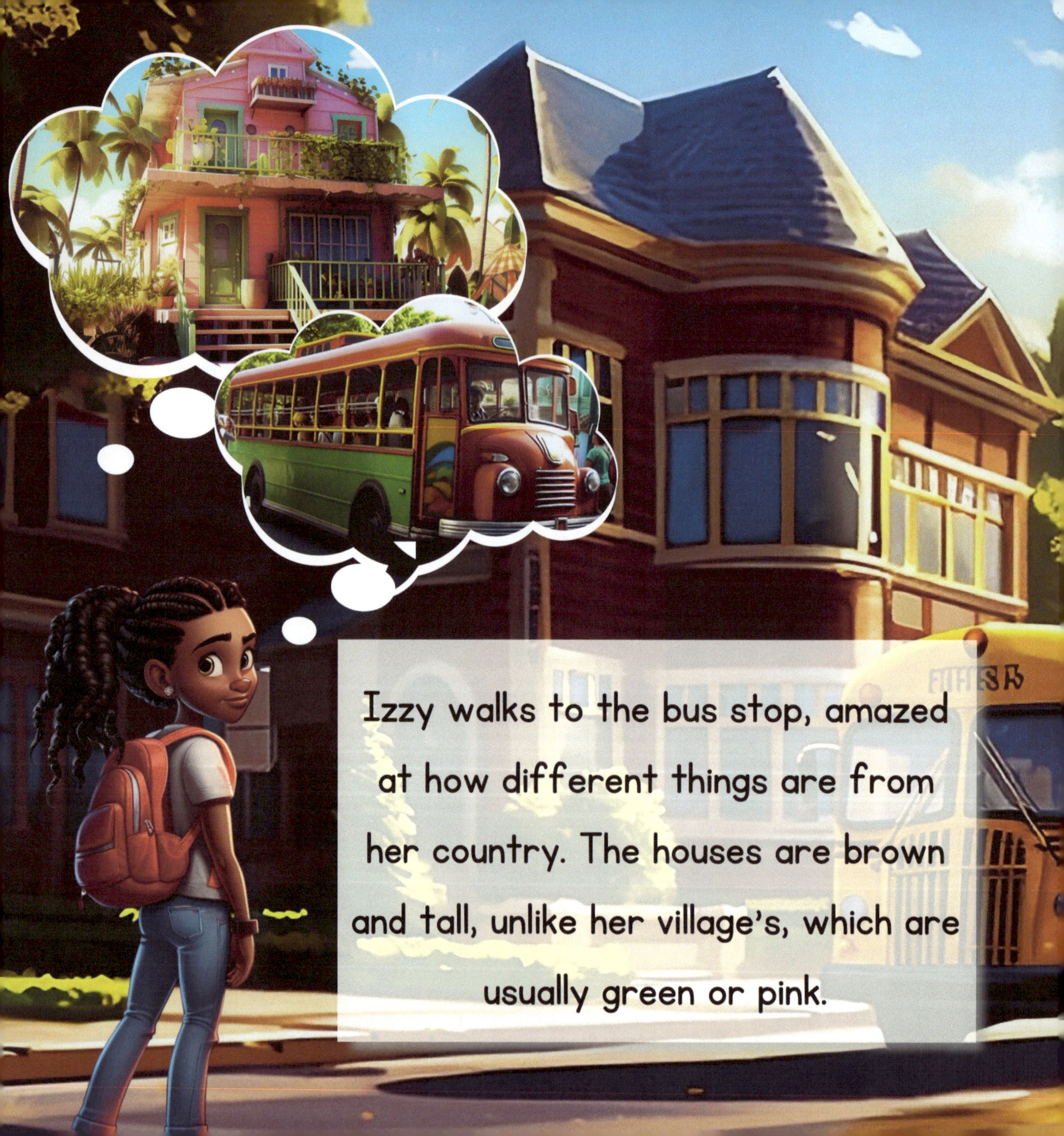

Izzy walks to the bus stop, amazed at how different things are from her country. The houses are brown and tall, unlike her village's, which are usually green or pink.

The school bus is yellow, and the bus driver quietly nods when she walks in. It's unlike the colourfully painted buses with a cheery bus conductor shouting, "Catch the 7:45 bus!" back in her village.

At school, she needs help finding her class. She sees a group of kids laughing and walking by. She is hoping that they can help her.

"HELLO! ALLYUH THINK YUH CUD SHOW ME, ME CLASS PLEASE?"
But they laugh and continue walking. Izzy convinces herself that they didn't hear her.

Izzy eventually finds her class, and her teacher asks her to introduce herself.
"HELLO, ME NAME IZZY. AND ME COME FROM GRENADA, A LIKKLE ISLAND IN THE CARIBBEAN. DEY CALL IT SPICE ISLE."

But once she starts talking, the kids stare at her, confused, and some even laugh.

At recess, Izzy walks over to a group of kids and asks if she can play. But once she starts talking again, they all start laughing.

When Izzy asks why they're laughing, one of the kids responds, "Because you talk funny!" They walk away, and their laughs become louder, and Izzy becomes sadder.

When Izzy gets home from school, her aunt asks her about her first day. Izzy tells her what happened and wishes she didn't sound so different from her classmates.

Her aunt encourages her to embrace her differences and her accent. Then she says,

"BE PROUD OF YOUR COUNTRY AND YOUR PEOPLE. YOUR HISTORY AND CULTURE ARE IN THE WAY YOU TALK. WHEN KIDS MAKE FUN OF YOUR ACCENT, USE THE MOMENT TO TEACH THEM ABOUT GRENADA."

It is a new day, and Izzy feels confident in who she is. Izzy's aunt and her friend from Jamaica make her feel proud to be Caribbean.

Izzy decides she won't let her classmates' opinions stop her from using her voice to ask class questions, make new friends, or talk.

Recess starts, and Izzy makes her way out to the schoolyard. She sees a group of kids again and decides to practice what her aunt says.

Some of the other kids hear Izzy and say,
"WHY DOES SHE TALK FUNNY?"
"SHE'S NOT TALKING FUNNY. THAT'S JUST HER COUNTRY'S ACCENT."

"JUST LIKE I HAVE AN ACCENT BECAUSE I SPEAK ITALIAN—I'M FROM ITALY! CIAO!!"
"AND ME ACCENT IS BECAUSE I AM FROM GRENADA. W'AP'NIN? SOMETIMES WE SPEAK CREOLE. ME TANTY SAID THAT THERE WAS A BATTLE BETWEEN THE ENGLISH AND FRENCH MEN FOR ME COUNTRY."

Izzy goes on to tell them that because of this battle, her country has a mixture of French and English words in their language. Izzy invites her new friends to her house to eat some Grenadian food and learn more about her country. She is happy!

Izzy and her friends come home to Soca music playing in the backyard, and her aunt is making Grenada's national dish, Oil Down. Her aunt greets them and says,
"ALLYUH 'W'AP'NIN?'"

Izzy looks at her new friends as if to say, "you know how to respond," and they all say,
"I DEY MAN!"
"I DEY MAN!"
"I DEY MAN!"
"I DEY MAN!"
"I DEY MAN!"

Izzy breathes a big sigh of relief as she snuggles into bed.
"TEDDY? AH GO SEE YUH IN DE 'MAWNING!"

Her new life in Canada is going well, and although she misses her village, she's excited about her new life here. For now, she cherishes the memories of her beautiful Spice Isle close to her heart.

"HELLO FRIENDS! READ MY SCHOOL REPORT AND GET TO KNOW ME COUNTRY!"
I ♥ GRENADA

MY COUNTRY REPORT

NAME OF COUNTRY- **GRENADA**

COUNTRY CAPITAL- **ST.GEORGES**

LANGUAGE/S - **ENGLISH & CREOLE**

This Creole language is a blend of English and African, French, and other Caribbean linguistic influences.

CURRENCY

Eastern Caribbean dollar (XCD)

IMPORTANT FACTS

- Independence day is February 7th, 1974.

- Grenada is often called the "Spice Isle" because it produces spices like nutmeg, cloves, cinnamon, and ginger.

- The Grenadian Carnival, known as "Spicemas," is a vibrant and colourful celebration that takes place in August.

- St. George's University: This prestigious international university is located in Grenada and offers programs in various fields, including medicine, veterinary medicine, business, and more.

MAIN INDUSTRIES

NUTMEG & MACE

TOURISM

AGRICULTURE

SOME OF GRENADA'S LOCAL LANGUAGE TERMINIOLOGY

AREDI

GRENADIANS SAY THIS TO SOMEONE WHEN THEY ARE READY TO GO SOMEWHERE OR LEAVE A PLACE.

CHOONGSIE

GRENADIANS USE THIS WORD WHEN THEY WANT SOMEONE O GIVE THEM A TINY PIECE OF SOMETHING.

E.G. GI MI A CHOONGSIE PIECE OF CAKE NAH?

DAN DAN

GRENADIANS USE THIS TERM FOR DESCRIBING SOMEONE'S OUTFIT BEING NICE OR FANCY.

E.G. YOU HAVE ON A NICE DAN DAN FOR CHURCH DEY BOY.

SHOOSHOO

GRENADIANS USE THIS TERM TO SAY SOMEONE IS WHISPERING OR SPEAKING QUIETLY IN SECRET.

E.G. WHAT YOU SHOOSHOOING ABOUT?

All of Our Books

Printed in the USA
CPSIA information can be obtained
at www.ICGtesting.com
LVHW062152300124
770372LV00002BA/56